Twenty One Pilots

FLYING HIGH TO SUCCESS, WEIRD AND INTERESTING FACTS ON THE BREAKOUT BAND

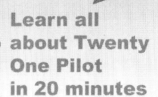

Learn all about Twenty One Pilot in 20 minutes

With Bern Bolo
The Bathroom Genius

D1595740

creating this book. However, they do not warrant or represent that the contents within are accurate due to the internet's rapidly changing nature. Although the Author and Publisher made all attempts to verify information, they do not assume any responsibility for errors, omissions, or contrary interpretation of the subject matter contained within as perceived slights of peoples, persons, organizations are unintentional and information contained within should not be used as a source of legal, business, accounting, financial, or other professional advice.

This book is unofficial and unauthorized. It is not authorized, approved, licensed, or endorsed by the aforementioned interests or any of their licensees.

About the Publisher
Epiphany Printing is a member of the **BLVNP**
Incorporated Group,
340 S. Lemon #6200, Walnut, CA 91789,
info@blvnp.com / legal@blvnp.com

Twenty One Pilots

*

*

Flying High to Success

*

*

Weird and Interesting Facts on the
Breakout Band

By Bern Bolo

ISBN: 978-1-68030-715-3

TABLE OF CONTENTS
***

FREE DOWNLOAD

 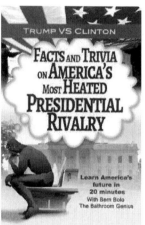

Know more about **CLINTON'S COMEBACK and TRUMP vs HILLARY** by reading the **FREE Chapters** when you sign up for <u>Bern Bolo's</u> mailing list!

I wish I found some better sounds no one's ever heard.

I wish I had a better voice that sang some better words.

I wish I found some chords in an order that is new.

I wish I didn't have to rhyme every time I sang.

--"Stressed Out", Twenty One Pilots

Introduction

Are you into an "alternative" alternative music? Then Twenty One Pilots is the band just right for you. Twenty One Pilots will show the anxiety of the millennium, the almost "lost" faith, the stressing of the mind and emotion, the hits and the misses, the longing for home, the brave upfront — all these elements are present in their lyrics and their melodies. Clearly, one cannot get enough of them. Twenty One Pilots will give us the high that we all need — good music and high spirits.

Metaphorically, I'm the man

But literally, I don't know what I'd do

"I'd live for you," and that's hard to do

--"Ride", Twenty One Pilots

The Twenty One Pilots

What is Twenty One Pilots?

If you happen to live under a rock, Twenty One Pilots is an electro-pop-rock indie band composed of members Tyler Joseph and Josh Dun. They have a unique style that garnered them the distinction of having a "Schizoid Pop" sound. The schizoid term is to describe their musical styling— they have songs which can be categorized as pop, rock, metal, ballad, among others.

Why are they the "next big thing?"

From their small beginnings in Columbus, Ohio, Twenty One Pilots are now ready to take on the world! Store them on your playlist to believe that Twenty One Pilots embodies the music you need in this world of weird disorder and tiring chaos.

The Beginning

Band's Name

Tyler Joseph came up with the band's name after studying the novel *All My Sons* written by Arthur Miller. Set in a war era, the novel *All my Sons* is about a businessman who sold faulty plane parts. The faulty plane parts eventually caused the deaths of 21 pilots during the war. A little tragic, isn't it? The dilemma of the story was just the inspiration in getting the band's name.

Original Band Members

The original band was formed in 2009 with members Tyler Joseph, Nick Thomas, and Chris Sahli. Nick and Chris left Twenty One Pilots in 2011 due to their busy schedules. Josh Dun joined Tyler to form the duo.

Facts about Tyler Joseph

Tyler Joseph was born on December 1, 1988. He hails from Columbus, Ohio.

He grew up with two brothers, Zack (also a singer) and Jay, and a sister, Madison. His mother, Kelly, was a math teacher while his father, Chris, was a coach at Worthington Christian High School during 1996–2005, and is a school's principal.

Tyler was homeschooled when he was young.

Tyler played basketball from a very young age. He became a point guard for Worthington Christian High School.

He rejected a basketball scholarship offer from Otterbein University and began playing music after finding an old keyboard in his closet.

He is married to Jenna Black. They wed last March 28, 2015 after being engaged since July 2014.

His first real exposure to music was the Christian hip hop group, DC Talk.

Joseph has a three-part tattoo which meant "something that saved his life." Everyone assumes that the ink deals with his Christian faith, Tyler indicated that he doesn't want the meaning of his tattoos spread across the web. If you want to know the meaning of the tattoo, Tyler is willing to tell you one-on-one if you decide to ask him (in person). Isn't that the coolest!

<u>Facts about Josh Dun</u>

Josh Dun was born in Columbus, Ohio on June 18, 1988. He has two sisters and a brother. He taught himself how to play drums when he was young.

Josh worked at the Guitar Center for three years.

In 2011, Josh went to a Twenty One Pilots show by the invitation of the then-drummer Chris Salih. He was impressed with the trio's performance. He then met the band's lead singer, Tyler Joseph, after the show. After a few days, Tyler and Josh began to spend time together and build their friendship.

Josh has an ink of a tree on his right arm. He prefers to tell people what the meaning of this tattoo in person. He wants the meaning to stay personal and desires for it not to go viral on the internet.

Before joining Twenty One Pilots, Josh Dun stood as the band's drummer before eventually joining the group. He was the drummer for House of Heroes before joining Twenty One Pilots.

Tyler and Josh Facts

Both Joseph and Josh have an "X" tattoo on their body to show their dedication to hometown fans in Columbus, Ohio. They both got their tattoos on stage during a hometown show at the Lifestyle Communities Pavilion on April 26, 2013. Tyler's X tattoo is on his right bicep while Josh's X is on his neck behind the right ear.

Although Joseph is not a big video game player, he said they love to play Mario Kart 64 on Nintendo to while away time on tours.

Both Tyler and Josh are devout Christians.

Twenty One Pilots is also known for doing covers of popular songs. In 2011, they did a cover of "Jar of Hearts", originally performed by Christina Perri.

Regarding their work, Twenty One Pilots employs a very collaborative process: Tyler is in charge of writing the lyrics and putting in melody while Josh checks and works the song out.

There are things we can do

But from the things that work there are only

two

And from the two that we choose to do

Peace will win

And fear will lose

There's faith, and there's sleep

We need to pick one please because

Faith is to be awake

--"Car Radio", Twenty One Pilots

Hits and Music

Twenty One Pilots released their first self-titled debut album on December 29, 2009. While releasing this record, the band members were Tyler Joseph, Nick Thomas, and Chris Sahli. During this time, Twenty One Pilots began touring their hometown, Columbus, Ohio.

In 2011, when Nick Thomas and Chris Sahli left the band, Twenty One Pilots released their second self-release, *Regional at Best*, with members Tyler Joseph and Josh Dun.

In November 2011, they played a sold out show (which is pretty great for an upcoming band at that time) at Columbus' Newport Music Hall attracting the attention of a dozen record labels.

Also in 2011, the duo also gave their fans two songs: "House of Gold" and a single entitled "Two."

In April 2012, at a jam-packed show at the Lifestyle Communities Pavilion, they announced their signing with a record company. Well, with a band like that, we all know that many record labels will fight over to get them. Twenty One Pilots ultimately decided that they would sign with Fueled by Ramen, a subsidiary of Atlantic Records.

It was on July 17, 2012, when they released their debut album with Fueled by Ramen recording in the form of a three-song EP, entitled *Three Songs*.

In August 2012, Twenty One Pilots embarked on a short tour with Neon Trees and Walk the Moon. Here, the band worked with Greg Wells, producer of Adele and

Katy Perry, on their first full-length album under Fueled by Ramen, *Vessel*. The album was later released on January 8, 2013.

Twenty One Pilots currently has their first radio hit in America, "Holding on to You", which has reached the 11th spot on the Billboard Alternative Songs chart.

So far, they have released four albums. Two were self-released: *Twenty One Pilots* (2009) and *Regional at Best* (2011). Having signed with Fueled by Ramen in 2013, they released two albums under the record company: *Vessel* (2013) and *Blurryface* (2015).

Some notable Youtube uploads of the bands are as follows:

Stressed Out which was uploaded last April 2015 has a stunning 220M views on Youtube.

The official music video "Holding on to You" was released on YouTube on November 12, 2012.

Other notable performances and appearances of our favorite duo are as follows:

In May 2013, Fall Out Boy announced that Twenty One Pilots will be touring as opening acts on the Save Rock and Roll Arena Tour the following Fall.

Tyler Joseph also participated and sang "O come, O come, Emmanuel" at Five14 Church's Christmas with the Stars in New Albany, Ohio. He also performed a "magic" segment with David McCreary for the show. Talk about talents!

As 2015 ushered in, the duo broke into the mainstream. They appeared at music festivals and other events all around the country, including Lollapalooza, Bonnaroo, Boston Calling, and Firefly.

As a result of these appearances, they took the show requests from different cities. This became the Quiet Is Violent World Tour, which began in September 2014.

Twenty One Pilots also performed at the 2014 MTV Movie Awards, singing out "Car Radio."

So far, *Blurryface* is their biggest ticket to fame. The track "Stressed Out" peaked at number 2 on the Billboard Hot 100, and number one on both Alternative Songs and Hot Rock Songs.

The band began the Blurryface World Tour last May 11, 2015 starting in Glasgow, Scotland. The US part of their tour started on September 8 that same year at Washington, D.C. Their tour covered the United States, Australia, South East Asia, Japan, and Europe.

Here are the tracks of the album Blurryface:

> Heavy Dirty Soul
>
> Stressed Out
>
> Ride
>
> Fairly Local
>
> Tear In My Heart
>
> Lane Boy
>
> The Judge
>
> Doubt

Polarize

We Don't Believe What's On T.V.

Message Man

Hometown

Not Today

Goner

Of course, once in the scene, recognitions will be given. You will be delighted to know that Twenty One Pilots won the iHeartRadio Music Awards – Alternative Rock Artist of the Year (2016). And as expected, "Stressed Out" won iHeartRadio Music Awards as the Alternative Rock Song of the Year.

Here are other nominations for our loved Twenty One Pilots:

> MTV Video Music Award – Artist to Watch (2013)
> MTV Europe Music Awards - Best Push Act (2013)
> AP Music Awards – Best Live Band (2014)
> AP Music Awards – Album of the Year (2014)
> AP Music Awards – Breakthrough Band (2014) - Nominated
> Josh Dun - AP Music Awards – Best Drummer (2014)
> AP Music Awards – Best Live Band (2015)
> AP Music Awards – Most Dedicated Fans (2015)
> AP Music Awards – Tumblr Fandom of the Year (2015)
> "Tear in My Heart" - Teen Choice Award - Choice Rock Song (2015)

The band canceled their 2015 European tour in the wake of the Paris terrorist attacks. On Twitter, Tyler sent out the following tweets:

"Not only were lives taken by senseless acts of violence, but the tragic event hit close.

"We had just been there the day before; me, Josh, our crew, my wife, playing a concert. I keep thinking, 'It could have been our show. It could have been our lighting and sound guy. It could have been our pit of fans.'

"Could I ever continue after that? Peace will win, and fear will lose,"

*But I know a thing or two about pain and
darkness
If it wasn't for this music, I don't know how
I would've fought this*

--"Lane Boy", Twenty One Pilots

The Logo

The Twenty One Pilots' logo will simply blow you
away. It looks like a broken "H." It is made up of
geometric shapes of three rectangles all inside one big
circle. Over the course of their career, the logo has
undergone several changes, and the interpretation given
to each will make you want to hear more about it.

Tyler Joseph designed the logo. If you want to know its
meaning, here's what he has to say about it.

> "It means Twenty One Pilots, the logo does.
> Why it means Twenty One Pilots, is it goes
> along with one of our songs called 'Kitchen
> Sink.' The whole concept of that song is that I
> feel that humans are always struggling all the
> time when it comes to purpose, trying to figure
> out their purpose is, what purpose even is,
> what's the point justifying your existence. A lot
> of kids and people my age struggle with 'what's
> the point,' and with the logo, what it really
> means is it's an encouragement. When someone

asks me what the logo means to me, the logo means something to me because I made it mean something to me. That's the point."

Tyler does not stop there, he continues with the explanation of their logo— and to hear him explain it is so inspiring.

"The point is that I created something that only I understand and whether or not I decide to disclose the meaning of it, that's the beginning of purpose for me. The meaning of purpose for me is by creating something if it be by writing lyrics, painting a picture, by expressing yourself through art, if it's photography or music or theater, or whatever it is. It doesn't have to be artistic, but if you create something, and only you know the meaning of it, that's the beginning of purpose for you. When you're in the room by yourself trying to decide whether to stay alive, you can tell yourself, 'I should probably stay alive because I'm the only one who knows the meaning of that thing,' so the logo is an encouragement for people to create. That's what it means."

I'm not evil to the core
What I shouldn't do I will fight
I know I'm emotional
What I wanna save I will try

--"Fairly Local", Twenty One Pilots

Weird Trivia AND Interesting Facts

Twenty One Pilots followers often show they are fans by holding up the middle and index fingers on their left hand, forming a "V." Then placing the right index finger horizontal behind it. This imitates the band's logo.

So, if you're a fan, you should be putting your fingers like this

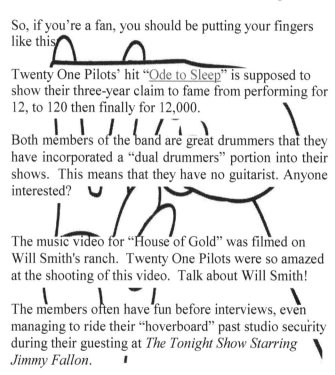

Twenty One Pilots' hit "Ode to Sleep" is supposed to show their three-year claim to fame from performing for 12, to 120 then finally for 12,000.

Both members of the band are great drummers that they have incorporated a "dual drummers" portion into their shows. This means that they have no guitarist. Anyone interested?

The music video for "House of Gold" was filmed on Will Smith's ranch. Twenty One Pilots were so amazed at the shooting of this video. Talk about Will Smith!

The members often have fun before interviews, even managing to ride their "hoverboard" past studio security during their guesting at *The Tonight Show Starring Jimmy Fallon.*

The band has been on the hot-seat for their views or lack of opinion about marriage and equality. When interviewed, Tyler has stated that they do not wish to comment on topics just so that they could sell songs like other artists.

Twenty One Pilots uses unique optical illusion patterns for their singles on Youtube and Wordpress. If you happen to like listening to Twenty One Pilots' audio streams, beware! The patterns are blurry and can cause tension migraine attacks.

Just in case you missed it, Twenty One Pilots included their family member in the filming of their music. Tyler and Josh's grandfathers were featured on their 2013 album cover for *"Vessel"*. This is even greater-- their families were featured in their 2015 music video for "Stressed Out." Go ahead, search it on Youtube!!

In one of their radio guesting, Twenty One Pilots dragged their entire entourage to serve as their backup singers. This is when they performed a mash-up of "Safe and Sound" and "Get Lucky."

The duo came up with a rather complex handshake for their "Stressed Out" music video. They uploaded this on Youtube.

The band was once surprised by Fall Out Boy and Panic! at the Disco when both bands appeared during their Tampa show in 2013.

During their shows, Josh does a backflip from the top of Tyler's piano. This was incorporated into their music video for "Holding On To You." Only this time, the dancers jumped from Josh's drums instead.

In one of their shows, Josh has played his drum set on top of a small platform held up by the audience.

Tyler always manages to incorporate climbing something into their shows. From his piano to speakers and even the support pillar in a mall in the Philippines.

Do you know that whenever they are asked about the first time they met, Josh and Tyler always comes up with a new story that is completely fictional?

Josh once pretended to be a new radio DJ Spooky Jim to interview Tyler in one of their radio guestings. They had a running gag about Josh being kicked out of the band.

Early in their career, the band used ski-masks as their gimmick in videos and live shows. Going into their 2015 "Blurryface" album, they started using face and body paint instead. Tyler specifically uses black paint on his hands and throat to symbolize his anxieties.

Aside from the ski-masks, another running gimmick on their music videos for their *"Vessel"* album is to have inaudible dialogue that is shown via subtitle.

The first line of the song "Tear In My Heart", "Anyong haseyo" is a Korean greeting. Yes! It is "Anyong haseyo!!"

Their first single "Stressed Out" from their "Blurryface" album got into the US Top-10 and is lodged between the songs of Justin Bieber and One Direction. The album itself has gone up to number 3 best selling on the charts.

Not only have they performed on major TV shows like *The Tonight Show Starring Jimmy Fallon* and the *MTV Music Awards*. Twenty One Pilots have also gone on stage for major events like the X-Games.

In spite of their sudden claim to fame, the duo remains humble and choose to spend their downtime back home, in Columbus, Ohio. Tyler even bought a home in their local town to share with his new wife, Jenna Black.

Believing that newlyweds should not be separated during the first year of marriage, Jenna will be touring with the band on their 58-date arena tour.

Their shows are very energetic and would always incorporate some form of audience participation. If you subscribe to their videos, you will see that fans are included in their music videos.

After signing up with Fueled by Ramen, the duo is still very cautious about keeping their identity and artistic freedom. Other big acts under the label are Fall Out Boy and Paramore.

On defining their genre, Tyler says, "There was a lot of pressure to find a genre and stick to it. People would tell me all the time, 'You can't be all things to everyone.' I would say, 'I'm not trying to be! I'm being what I want to be for myself.'"

Tyler created the character Blurryface specifically for the album of the same name. He is meant to show his insecurities and is meant to go away when the tour for the album ends and a new one comes out.

Although their songs often have serious themes told in an upbeat way, the guys can't seem to take their interviews seriously. They would fool around and even role-play. They would even invent stories. Haha!

The guys have become so famous that there are a lot of "fan-fiction" on them. Some are fantastic while others would go as far as having a romantic relationship between the two male members of the band, and even some are very sensual stories. Talk about range!

The duo says that they might consider adding other members to the group, but they could not imagine not performing without each other. Josh even said that if he ever considers going solo, he would still have Tyler perform the vocals for all of his songs.

They encourage their followers to be creative and even started the concept of showcasing their work on their Twitter account and called it #fanartfridays.

Their dedication to their fans went so deep that they even had matching tattoos drawn on them in the middle of their show, on stage.

Likewise, their fans are so enthusiastic that they held New Year's Day Blurryface launch parties to celebrate the album's launch.

One other time the two had to get tattoos on stage was when they conducted a poll where the loser would have the winner's name tattooed on his body. The Twitter poll ended in a tie which is why they ended up tattooing the other person's name on each other.

Remember the moment

You know exactly where you're going,

'Cause the next moment,

Before you know it, time is slowing

--"Holding On To You", Twenty One Pilots

Closing In On Twenty One Pilots

So there you have it, your rundown on the Twenty One Pilots. Rolling Stones call them the biggest breakout of the century. Their music embodies the millennial anxiety, the tiredness of the people. Some would even say that they're weird particularly when it comes to the explanation of their logo or the way that they fabricate stories in every interview. Well, there's that, but also, there's the music. After all, we all know that they are Christians, and they have a solid faith. Let's just call them, Twenty One Pilots.

REFERENCES

https://twitter.com/twentyonepilots

https://www.youtube.com/watch?v=l0oovgCbBks

https://www.youtube.com/watch?v=zYcQ2d4v7sk

https://www.youtube.com/watch?v=l0oovgCbBks

https://www.youtube.com/watch?v=uKRRxrbkiVo

https://www.youtube.com/watch?v=ZxTnmHbR8-g

https://www.youtube.com/watch?v=tVYCCYKTqWQ

https://www.youtube.com/watch?v=puEX9On-tW4

https://www.youtube.com/watch?v=R_HDifqMHSY

https://www.youtube.com/user/twentyonepilots

http://www.azlyrics.com/t/twentyonepilots.html

https://www.youtube.com/watch?v=pXRviuL6vMY

https://www.youtube.com/watch?v=3P8HjBy84g

https://en.wikipedia.org/wiki/Twenty_One_Pilots#Awards

https://twitter.com/tylerrjoseph?ref_src=twsrc%5Etfw

https://www.youtube.com/watch?v=eZxg5jgjA9U&ebc=
ANyPxKqRUZJ7y8RpKnQvqXCiCXnk0VPQQ0G7BFl
zVNQHQxvPWinGDy41F835msbaoVmWWA8JvWdP
x4Ur2AepqZG8COpcXTj0WA

https://www.youtube.com/watch?v=CtIhqEBVFpE&ebc
=ANyPxKpWgdorMfD9dBRs3NLxupPlTlmUH3om0ty
gKZY_l6DAOocL2iVX05xP2NUNg4iA26_URUWjrC6
BqCZvbBQ8CZk_02o5AA

https://www.youtube.com/watch?v=Pmv8aQKO6k0&eb
c=ANyPxKo4TgWSA4CWUoAult-
BSt7pYl3WLbSlvzIYM-
2ZdLIfR_u7bLHMnpFL4wFk0pzPEfa5D9EvbFmwkYI
8_gbD3B3-RrY5oQ

http://www.rollingstone.com/music/features/twenty-one-
pilots-inside-the-biggest-new-band-of-the-past-year-
20160114

https://www.youtube.com/watch?v=2OnO3UXFZdE&in
dex=7&list=PL8E828464E67B2CE5

https://en.wikipedia.org/wiki/Twenty_One_Pilots#Music
al_style_and_influence
https://www.youtube.com/watch?v=pXRviuL6vMY&eb
c=ANyPxKqJPYV58BcpJP6cR5_1tzvszZ8gl9zqi4HZN
0RMPx45ASAbG0qG1cbxEXOYthwIv7fO5osKCJwLII
KlPhwThz2Z4q05BQ
http://www.rollingstone.com/music/news/13-things-we-
learned-hanging-out-with-twenty-one-pilots-
20160120?page=4
http://www.rollingstone.com/music/news/13-things-we-
learned-hanging-out-with-twenty-one-pilots-20160120
http://www.rollingstone.com/music/news/13-things-we-
learned-hanging-out-with-twenty-one-pilots-20160120
http://www.rollingstone.com/music/news/13-things-we-
learned-hanging-out-with-twenty-one-pilots-20160120
http://www.rollingstone.com/music/news/13-things-we-
learned-hanging-out-with-twenty-one-pilots-20160120
http://www.rollingstone.com/music/news/13-things-we-
learned-hanging-out-with-twenty-one-pilots-20160120
http://www.rollingstone.com/music/news/13-things-we-
learned-hanging-out-with-twenty-one-pilots-20160120
http://www.rollingstone.com/music/news/13-things-we-
learned-hanging-out-with-twenty-one-pilots-20160120
http://www.rollingstone.com/music/news/13-things-we-
learned-hanging-out-with-twenty-one-pilots-20160120
http://www.rollingstone.com/music/features/twenty-one-
pilots-inside-the-biggest-new-band-of-the-past-year-
20160114
https://www.youtube.com/watch?v=nky4me4NP70&ebc
=ANyPxKocP9FSvbck8Tfw1MwxGH18rXiJp9wz2XG9
TGDx2JJiRDwN8W9FF_RncaTkcsNP-
6Qrm5vx7pnn1aBdfICXNpmBQsqKxA

Can't get enough of **CLINTON'S COMEBACK and TRUMP vs HILLARY**?

Make sure you sign up for my blog to find out more..!

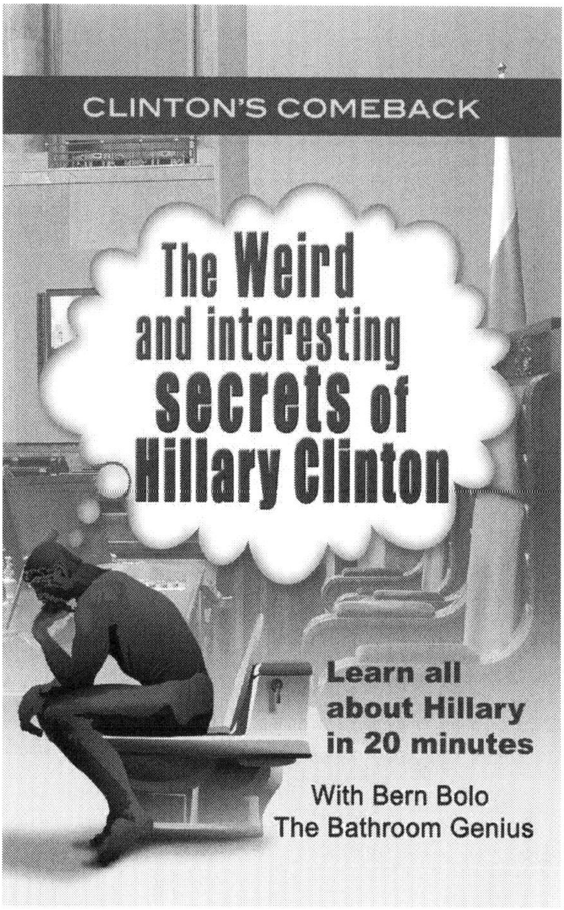
CLINTON'S COMEBACK
The Weird
and interesting
secrets of
Hillary Clinton
Learn all
about Hillary
in 20 minutes
With Bern Bolo
The Bathroom Genius

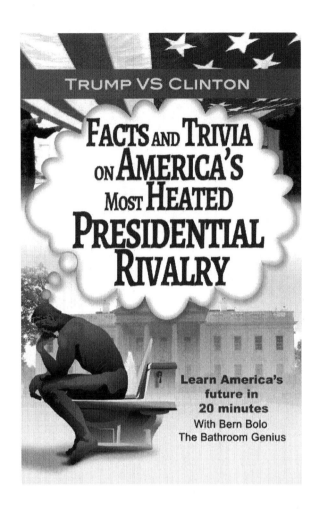

Get this **bonus chapters** when you sign up
at <u>Bern Bolo's</u> mailing list!

Know More About Hillary Clnton!

After losing the 2008 nomination to Barrack Obama, she is now back to her aim of being the first female president of the United States.

With huge experience in politics and the public office, she wants to be "a champion" of Americans.

Get to know Hillary Clinton: from her personal life to her love life, political standpoints and even her future plans for the country.

A PREVIEW of WEIRD and INTERESTING SECRESTS you can get from this trivia & facts book:

- Hillary's history.
- Her successes.
- Rising above her controversies.
- Weird and interesting facts about Hillary Clinton.
- What she is fighting for.
- What her secret plans for the country are.

Decide if she will have your vote.

Look for **CLINTON'S COMEBACK: Weird and Interesting Secrets of Hillary Clinton** On Amazon

**Know More…..Who do you think will
WIN this 2016th Election?**

Donald Trump wants to "make America great again" while Hillary Clinton wants to "become America's champion."

Who will you go for?

In this trivia book, we will explore how these candidates compare to each other. From their personal to professional lives, we will give you all there is know about both of these very controversial figures. Most importantly, we will give you their stand and viewpoints on very crucial issues on the country, revealing their respective platforms and plans for America along the way!

Important lessons you learn from the summary

- A comparison of Hillary and Donald's personal and professional lives
- The platform and views of both candidates and their future plans for the country

The future of the American people lies in the hands of whoever gets elected this coming election. Get to know your candidates and choose wisely!

Look for **TRUMP VS. CLINTON: Facts a nd Tri via on Ameri ca's Mo s t Hea ted Presidential Rivalry** On Amazon

About the Author

Bern Bolo

Two years ago, I was so ignorant that I did not even know how to copy-and-paste. I did not know what net income and gross profit were or what a profit cycle meant. BUT...

My spirit kept leading me to the world of business. I wanted to be in it so much and I didn't know how. Yet, it did not matter. One of the cardinal things that I have learned from all my experiences: once you have the courage and the right drive, you are halfway to your dreams.

At first, I just dreamed of becoming a businessperson. I strived hard, and by reading LOTS and lots of business books, like Zero to One, The One Minute Manager, Cashflow Quadrant, Unfair Advantage, and more, I received epiphany after epiphany. Now, my dreams are a reality. Now, I am in the arena.

Only TWO YEARS later, I have established a profitable business and I have provided opportunities to many people, who are now working for me.

Sometimes, I look back and connect the dots of my past to those of my present. I have accomplished what I used to think was impossible to reach. And that never fails to amaze me. Who would have thought that reading these books could change my life? Books, indeed, are one of the most powerful things a man can hold.

I AM SO LUCKY to realise that soon enough. I was only dreaming many years before.

For my reader, I wish you greater success than I have ever had, in even less time. I wish for Epiphany Printing to open your eyes and mind, and fortify your will and spirit, so that you, too, can see how abundant the world is…

So that you, too, can see the opportunities that you never thought existed and realize that they are right there, next to you.

Through my writings, let your spirit wake up. Be who you want to be. You are so lucky. You always have been. Keep thinking that, and you will get luckier. :)

Made in the USA
Middletown, DE
23 March 2018